50 Cozy Breakfast Ideas for Winter Mornings

By: Kelly Johnson

Table of Contents

- Warm Cinnamon Oatmeal with Apples
- Maple Pecan Pancakes
- Creamy Avocado Toast with Poached Eggs
- Sweet Potato Hash with Sausage
- French Toast Casserole
- Hot Chocolate Smoothie
- Baked Eggs in Avocado
- Cinnamon Roll Waffles
- Apple and Pear Crumble
- Savory Breakfast Burritos
- Cranberry Almond Scones
- Gingerbread Pancakes
- Spiced Chai Latte Oatmeal
- Egg and Cheese Breakfast Muffins
- Lemon Ricotta Pancakes
- Warm Banana Nut Quinoa
- Pumpkin Spice French Toast
- Hot Cocoa Porridge
- Sausage and Egg Skillet
- Baked Apple Cinnamon French Toast
- Sweet Cinnamon Roll Casserole
- Winter Citrus Salad with Yogurt
- Warm Vanilla Chia Pudding
- Creamy Coconut Rice Pudding
- Spicy Breakfast Tacos with Salsa
- Pear and Almond Butter Toast
- Cranberry Orange Muffins
- Poached Eggs with Roasted Potatoes
- Bacon, Spinach, and Cheese Croissants
- Hot Spiced Apple Cider with Breakfast Biscuits
- Mushroom and Swiss Omelette
- Oatmeal with Roasted Winter Squash
- Hazelnut Coffee Cake
- Warm Apple Cinnamon Polenta
- Nutella-Stuffed Pancakes

- Cream Cheese-Stuffed Belgian Waffles
- Buttermilk Biscuits with Gravy
- Warm Cinnamon Sugar Donuts
- Almond Joy Smoothie Bowl
- Roasted Pears with Greek Yogurt and Honey
- Savory Avocado and Spinach Smoothie
- Maple Bacon and Cheddar Breakfast Quiche
- Lemon and Blueberry Ricotta Pancakes
- Hot Buttered Rum Oatmeal
- Toasted Bagels with Smoked Salmon
- Cranberry Walnut Granola with Yogurt
- Chia Seed Pudding with Ginger Pear Compote
- Breakfast Potatoes with Sweet Bell Peppers
- Hot Apple and Almond Butter Slices
- Cinnamon Spiced Dutch Baby Pancakes

Warm Cinnamon Oatmeal with Apples

Ingredients:

- 1 cup of rolled oats
- 2 cups of milk or water
- 1/2 teaspoon of ground cinnamon
- 1 apple, peeled, cored, and chopped
- 1 tablespoon of honey or maple syrup (optional)
- A pinch of salt

Instructions:

1. In a pot, combine oats, milk (or water), and a pinch of salt. Bring to a boil.
2. Lower the heat and simmer for about 5-7 minutes, stirring occasionally.
3. Add cinnamon, chopped apples, and honey or syrup (if desired). Stir to combine.
4. Continue cooking for 2-3 minutes until apples soften.
5. Serve warm, topped with additional cinnamon or nuts if preferred.

Maple Pecan Pancakes

Ingredients:

- 1 cup of all-purpose flour
- 1 tablespoon of sugar
- 1 teaspoon of baking powder
- 1/2 teaspoon of baking soda
- 1/4 teaspoon of salt
- 1 cup of buttermilk
- 1 egg
- 1 tablespoon of melted butter
- 1/4 cup of chopped pecans
- Maple syrup for serving

Instructions:

1. In a large bowl, whisk together flour, sugar, baking powder, baking soda, and salt.
2. In a separate bowl, whisk together buttermilk, egg, and melted butter.
3. Pour the wet ingredients into the dry ingredients and stir until just combined.
4. Fold in the chopped pecans.
5. Heat a griddle or pan over medium heat and lightly grease it.
6. Pour 1/4 cup of batter onto the griddle for each pancake. Cook until bubbles form on the surface, then flip and cook the other side until golden brown.
7. Serve with maple syrup and extra pecans.

Creamy Avocado Toast with Poached Eggs

Ingredients:

- 2 slices of whole-grain or sourdough bread
- 1 ripe avocado
- 2 eggs
- Salt and pepper to taste
- Red pepper flakes (optional)
- Fresh herbs for garnish (optional)

Instructions:

1. Toast the slices of bread to your desired crispiness.
2. Mash the avocado in a bowl and season with salt and pepper.
3. Poach the eggs by gently cracking them into simmering water and cooking for 3-4 minutes until the whites are set.
4. Spread the mashed avocado onto the toast.
5. Place a poached egg on top of each slice and sprinkle with red pepper flakes and fresh herbs if desired.

Sweet Potato Hash with Sausage

Ingredients:

- 2 medium sweet potatoes, peeled and diced
- 1 tablespoon of olive oil
- 1/2 onion, diced
- 2 sausage links, cooked and crumbled
- 1 bell pepper, diced
- 1 teaspoon of paprika
- Salt and pepper to taste
- Fresh parsley for garnish

Instructions:

1. Heat olive oil in a large skillet over medium heat.
2. Add the diced sweet potatoes and cook, stirring occasionally, for about 10 minutes until they start to soften.
3. Add the onion, bell pepper, and paprika, and cook for another 5-7 minutes until the vegetables are tender.
4. Stir in the crumbled sausage and cook for an additional 2-3 minutes.
5. Season with salt and pepper and garnish with fresh parsley before serving.

French Toast Casserole

Ingredients:

- 8 slices of bread (preferably stale)
- 4 large eggs
- 2 cups of milk
- 1/4 cup of brown sugar
- 1 teaspoon of vanilla extract
- 1 teaspoon of ground cinnamon
- Pinch of salt
- Powdered sugar for dusting
- Maple syrup for serving

Instructions:

1. Preheat the oven to 350°F (175°C) and grease a baking dish.
2. Cut the bread into cubes and arrange it in the baking dish.
3. In a bowl, whisk together eggs, milk, brown sugar, vanilla, cinnamon, and salt.
4. Pour the egg mixture over the bread cubes and press down to ensure the bread is soaked.
5. Bake for 40-45 minutes until the casserole is golden and set.
6. Dust with powdered sugar and serve with maple syrup.

Hot Chocolate Smoothie

Ingredients:

- 1 banana
- 1/2 cup of milk (or dairy-free alternative)
- 1 tablespoon of cocoa powder
- 1 tablespoon of peanut butter (optional)
- 1 tablespoon of honey or maple syrup
- Ice cubes

Instructions:

1. Blend the banana, milk, cocoa powder, peanut butter, honey, and ice cubes until smooth.
2. Pour into a glass and serve immediately for a creamy, chocolatey breakfast treat.

Baked Eggs in Avocado

Ingredients:

- 2 ripe avocados
- 4 small eggs
- Salt and pepper to taste
- Fresh herbs for garnish (optional)

Instructions:

1. Preheat your oven to 425°F (220°C).
2. Cut the avocados in half and remove the pits. Scoop out a bit of flesh to make room for the eggs.
3. Place the avocado halves on a baking sheet and crack an egg into each half.
4. Season with salt and pepper.
5. Bake for 12-15 minutes until the egg whites are set.
6. Garnish with fresh herbs and serve.

Cinnamon Roll Waffles

Ingredients:

- 1 can of cinnamon rolls (8 count)
- 1 tablespoon of melted butter
- Maple syrup for serving

Instructions:

1. Preheat the waffle iron according to the manufacturer's instructions.
2. Place the cinnamon rolls in the waffle iron and close the lid.
3. Cook for 2-3 minutes or until golden brown and crispy.
4. Drizzle with melted butter and maple syrup before serving.

Apple and Pear Crumble

Ingredients:

- 2 apples, peeled and sliced
- 2 pears, peeled and sliced
- 1/2 cup of rolled oats
- 1/4 cup of flour
- 1/4 cup of brown sugar
- 1/2 teaspoon of ground cinnamon
- 1/4 cup of butter, cubed

Instructions:

1. Preheat the oven to 375°F (190°C).
2. In a baking dish, combine the apple and pear slices.
3. In a separate bowl, mix the oats, flour, brown sugar, and cinnamon.
4. Add the cubed butter and use your fingers to crumble the mixture over the fruit.
5. Bake for 30-35 minutes until the topping is golden and the fruit is tender.
6. Serve warm with a scoop of vanilla ice cream if desired.

Savory Breakfast Burritos

Ingredients:

- 4 large flour tortillas
- 6 large eggs, scrambled
- 1/2 cup of cooked sausage, crumbled (optional)
- 1/2 cup of shredded cheese (cheddar or Monterey Jack)
- 1/4 cup of diced onions
- 1/4 cup of diced bell peppers
- 1/4 cup of salsa or hot sauce
- Salt and pepper to taste
- Fresh cilantro for garnish (optional)

Instructions:

1. In a skillet, sauté the diced onions and bell peppers until soft.
2. In a separate pan, scramble the eggs and season with salt and pepper.
3. Warm the tortillas in the microwave or on a griddle.
4. Layer scrambled eggs, sautéed onions, bell peppers, cooked sausage, and shredded cheese in the center of each tortilla.
5. Drizzle with salsa or hot sauce and roll up tightly.
6. Serve with a sprinkle of fresh cilantro.

Cranberry Almond Scones

Ingredients:

- 2 cups of all-purpose flour
- 1/2 cup of sugar
- 1 tablespoon of baking powder
- 1/4 teaspoon of salt
- 1/2 cup of cold butter, cubed
- 1/2 cup of dried cranberries
- 1/4 cup of slivered almonds
- 1/2 cup of heavy cream
- 1 large egg
- 1 teaspoon of vanilla extract

Instructions:

1. Preheat the oven to 400°F (200°C) and line a baking sheet with parchment paper.
2. In a bowl, combine flour, sugar, baking powder, and salt.
3. Cut in the cold butter until the mixture resembles coarse crumbs.
4. Stir in the cranberries and almonds.
5. In a separate bowl, whisk together the cream, egg, and vanilla extract.
6. Add the wet ingredients to the dry ingredients and mix until just combined.
7. Turn the dough out onto a floured surface and shape it into a round disk.
8. Cut into wedges and bake for 18-20 minutes, until golden brown.
9. Serve warm with butter or jam.

Gingerbread Pancakes

Ingredients:

- 1 1/2 cups of all-purpose flour
- 2 tablespoons of brown sugar
- 2 teaspoons of ground ginger
- 1 teaspoon of ground cinnamon
- 1/2 teaspoon of ground cloves
- 1 teaspoon of baking powder
- 1/2 teaspoon of baking soda
- 1/2 teaspoon of salt
- 1 egg
- 1 cup of milk
- 1/4 cup of molasses
- 2 tablespoons of melted butter
- 1 teaspoon of vanilla extract

Instructions:

1. In a large bowl, whisk together flour, sugar, ginger, cinnamon, cloves, baking powder, baking soda, and salt.
2. In a separate bowl, whisk together the egg, milk, molasses, melted butter, and vanilla extract.
3. Add the wet ingredients to the dry ingredients and stir until combined.
4. Heat a griddle or pan over medium heat and lightly grease it.
5. Pour 1/4 cup of batter onto the griddle for each pancake. Cook until bubbles form on the surface, then flip and cook the other side until golden brown.
6. Serve with maple syrup or whipped cream.

Spiced Chai Latte Oatmeal

Ingredients:

- 1 cup of rolled oats
- 2 cups of milk (or dairy-free alternative)
- 1/2 teaspoon of ground cinnamon
- 1/4 teaspoon of ground cardamom
- 1/4 teaspoon of ground ginger
- 1/8 teaspoon of ground cloves
- 1 tablespoon of honey or maple syrup
- Chopped nuts or dried fruit for topping (optional)

Instructions:

1. In a medium saucepan, combine oats, milk, cinnamon, cardamom, ginger, and cloves.
2. Bring to a boil, then reduce heat and simmer for 5-7 minutes, stirring occasionally.
3. Once the oats are tender, stir in honey or syrup to sweeten.
4. Serve topped with your favorite nuts or dried fruit for added texture.

Egg and Cheese Breakfast Muffins

Ingredients:

- 6 large eggs
- 1/2 cup of shredded cheese (cheddar, mozzarella, or your favorite)
- 1/4 cup of diced bell peppers
- 1/4 cup of diced onions
- Salt and pepper to taste
- Fresh herbs for garnish (optional)

Instructions:

1. Preheat the oven to 375°F (190°C) and grease a muffin tin.
2. In a bowl, whisk together eggs, cheese, bell peppers, onions, salt, and pepper.
3. Pour the egg mixture into the muffin cups, filling each about 3/4 full.
4. Bake for 12-15 minutes, or until the eggs are set and lightly golden.
5. Serve warm, garnished with fresh herbs if desired.

Lemon Ricotta Pancakes

Ingredients:

- 1 cup of all-purpose flour
- 1 tablespoon of sugar
- 1 teaspoon of baking powder
- 1/2 teaspoon of baking soda
- 1/4 teaspoon of salt
- 1 cup of ricotta cheese
- 1/2 cup of milk
- 1 large egg
- 1 tablespoon of lemon zest
- 1 teaspoon of vanilla extract

Instructions:

1. In a large bowl, whisk together flour, sugar, baking powder, baking soda, and salt.
2. In a separate bowl, whisk together ricotta, milk, egg, lemon zest, and vanilla.
3. Add the wet ingredients to the dry ingredients and stir until just combined.
4. Heat a griddle or pan over medium heat and lightly grease it.
5. Pour 1/4 cup of batter onto the griddle for each pancake. Cook until bubbles form on the surface, then flip and cook the other side until golden brown.
6. Serve with syrup or fresh berries.

Warm Banana Nut Quinoa

Ingredients:

- 1/2 cup of quinoa, rinsed
- 1 cup of milk (or dairy-free alternative)
- 1 ripe banana, mashed
- 1/4 cup of chopped walnuts
- 1 tablespoon of maple syrup
- 1/2 teaspoon of ground cinnamon
- A pinch of salt

Instructions:

1. In a saucepan, combine quinoa, milk, mashed banana, and cinnamon. Bring to a boil.
2. Reduce the heat and simmer for about 15 minutes until the quinoa is tender and the liquid is absorbed.
3. Stir in walnuts, salt, and maple syrup.
4. Serve warm for a hearty, nutritious breakfast.

Pumpkin Spice French Toast

Ingredients:

- 4 slices of bread (preferably thick-cut)
- 1/2 cup of canned pumpkin
- 2 large eggs
- 1/2 cup of milk
- 1 teaspoon of cinnamon
- 1/2 teaspoon of ground ginger
- 1/4 teaspoon of ground nutmeg
- 1/4 teaspoon of vanilla extract
- Butter for frying
- Maple syrup for serving

Instructions:

1. In a bowl, whisk together eggs, milk, pumpkin, cinnamon, ginger, nutmeg, and vanilla extract.
2. Dip each slice of bread into the egg mixture, making sure both sides are coated.
3. Heat a skillet over medium heat and melt butter.
4. Fry the bread slices until golden brown on both sides, about 3-4 minutes per side.
5. Serve with maple syrup and a sprinkle of cinnamon.

Hot Cocoa Porridge

Ingredients:

- 1 cup of rolled oats
- 2 cups of milk (or dairy-free alternative)
- 2 tablespoons of cocoa powder
- 1 tablespoon of sugar or maple syrup
- 1/4 teaspoon of vanilla extract
- Marshmallows for topping (optional)

Instructions:

1. In a saucepan, combine oats, milk, cocoa powder, sugar, and vanilla extract.
2. Bring to a boil, then reduce heat and simmer for 5-7 minutes, stirring occasionally.
3. Once the porridge is creamy and the oats are tender, remove from heat.
4. Serve topped with marshmallows for a cozy treat.

Sausage and Egg Skillet

Ingredients:

- 2 sausage links, crumbled
- 4 large eggs
- 1/2 cup of diced bell peppers
- 1/2 cup of diced onions
- 1/2 cup of shredded cheese (cheddar or mozzarella)
- Salt and pepper to taste
- Fresh herbs for garnish (optional)

Instructions:

1. Heat a skillet over medium heat and cook the sausage until browned and crumbled.
2. Add diced bell peppers and onions to the skillet and sauté until soft.
3. Push the sausage and vegetables to the side and crack the eggs into the skillet.
4. Cook the eggs to your preferred doneness, either sunny-side-up or scrambled.
5. Sprinkle cheese over the top and let it melt. Season with salt and pepper.
6. Garnish with fresh herbs and serve warm.

Baked Apple Cinnamon French Toast

Ingredients:

- 4 slices of bread (preferably thick-cut)
- 2 apples, peeled and sliced
- 1 teaspoon of cinnamon
- 1/2 teaspoon of nutmeg
- 2 large eggs
- 1/2 cup of milk
- 1 tablespoon of brown sugar
- 1 teaspoon of vanilla extract
- Butter for greasing

Instructions:

1. Preheat the oven to 350°F (175°C) and grease a baking dish with butter.
2. Arrange the bread slices in the baking dish and top with apple slices.
3. In a bowl, whisk together eggs, milk, brown sugar, cinnamon, nutmeg, and vanilla.
4. Pour the egg mixture over the bread and apples, making sure the bread is soaked.
5. Bake for 30-35 minutes, or until golden and cooked through.
6. Serve warm with syrup or powdered sugar.

Sweet Cinnamon Roll Casserole

Ingredients:

- 1 can of cinnamon roll dough (with icing)
- 4 large eggs
- 1 cup of milk
- 1/4 cup of brown sugar
- 1 teaspoon of cinnamon
- 1/2 teaspoon of vanilla extract

Instructions:

1. Preheat the oven to 350°F (175°C) and grease a casserole dish.
2. Cut the cinnamon rolls into quarters and place them in the casserole dish.
3. In a bowl, whisk together eggs, milk, brown sugar, cinnamon, and vanilla.
4. Pour the egg mixture over the cinnamon rolls, making sure they are evenly soaked.
5. Bake for 25-30 minutes, or until golden brown.
6. Drizzle the included icing over the casserole and serve warm.

Winter Citrus Salad with Yogurt

Ingredients:

- 2 oranges, peeled and sliced
- 1 grapefruit, peeled and sliced
- 1/2 cup of pomegranate seeds
- 1/2 cup of Greek yogurt
- 1 tablespoon of honey
- Fresh mint leaves for garnish (optional)

Instructions:

1. Arrange the orange and grapefruit slices in a serving bowl.
2. Sprinkle pomegranate seeds over the citrus.
3. In a small bowl, mix Greek yogurt and honey together.
4. Serve the citrus salad topped with a dollop of yogurt and garnish with fresh mint.

Warm Vanilla Chia Pudding

Ingredients:

- 1/4 cup of chia seeds
- 1 cup of milk (or dairy-free alternative)
- 1 teaspoon of vanilla extract
- 1 tablespoon of maple syrup
- Fresh berries or nuts for topping

Instructions:

1. In a bowl, combine chia seeds, milk, vanilla extract, and maple syrup.
2. Stir well and let sit in the fridge for at least 4 hours or overnight to thicken.
3. Once set, stir again and serve topped with fresh berries or nuts for crunch.

Creamy Coconut Rice Pudding

Ingredients:

- 1 cup of cooked rice
- 1 can of coconut milk (14 oz)
- 1/4 cup of sugar
- 1/4 teaspoon of vanilla extract
- A pinch of cinnamon
- Shredded coconut for garnish (optional)

Instructions:

1. In a saucepan, combine cooked rice, coconut milk, sugar, vanilla, and cinnamon.
2. Heat over medium heat, stirring constantly, until the mixture is thick and creamy (about 15 minutes).
3. Serve warm, topped with shredded coconut if desired.

Spicy Breakfast Tacos with Salsa

Ingredients:

- 4 small tortillas
- 4 large eggs
- 1/2 cup of cooked sausage (or chorizo)
- 1/4 cup of diced onions
- 1/4 cup of diced tomatoes
- 1 jalapeño, sliced (optional)
- Fresh cilantro for garnish
- Salsa for serving

Instructions:

1. Scramble the eggs in a skillet over medium heat, and season with salt and pepper.
2. In another pan, cook the sausage or chorizo until browned.
3. Warm the tortillas and fill each with eggs, sausage, onions, and tomatoes.
4. Top with jalapeños and cilantro, and serve with salsa on the side.

Pear and Almond Butter Toast

Ingredients:

- 2 slices of whole-grain bread
- 2 tablespoons of almond butter
- 1 pear, sliced thinly
- Honey for drizzling
- Cinnamon for sprinkling

Instructions:

1. Toast the bread slices to your desired crispness.
2. Spread almond butter over the toasted bread.
3. Top with pear slices, drizzle with honey, and sprinkle with cinnamon.
4. Serve immediately as a quick and nutritious breakfast.

Cranberry Orange Muffins

Ingredients:

- 1 1/2 cups of all-purpose flour
- 1 teaspoon of baking powder
- 1/2 teaspoon of baking soda
- 1/2 teaspoon of salt
- 1/2 cup of sugar
- 1/4 cup of orange juice
- 1/2 cup of milk
- 1/4 cup of vegetable oil
- 1 large egg
- 1 cup of fresh cranberries

Instructions:

1. Preheat the oven to 350°F (175°C) and line a muffin tin with paper liners.
2. In a large bowl, whisk together flour, baking powder, baking soda, salt, and sugar.
3. In another bowl, combine orange juice, milk, oil, and egg.
4. Stir the wet ingredients into the dry ingredients until just combined.
5. Gently fold in the cranberries.
6. Fill each muffin cup 3/4 full and bake for 18-20 minutes, or until golden.

Poached Eggs with Roasted Potatoes

Ingredients:

- 4 large eggs
- 2 cups of diced potatoes
- 1 tablespoon of olive oil
- 1 teaspoon of paprika
- Salt and pepper to taste
- Fresh parsley for garnish

Instructions:

1. Preheat the oven to 400°F (200°C).
2. Toss diced potatoes with olive oil, paprika, salt, and pepper.
3. Spread the potatoes on a baking sheet and roast for 25-30 minutes, flipping halfway through.
4. While the potatoes roast, poach the eggs by simmering water in a pan and gently cracking eggs into the water. Cook for 4-5 minutes for soft yolks.
5. Serve the poached eggs over the roasted potatoes and garnish with fresh parsley.

Bacon, Spinach, and Cheese Croissants

Ingredients:

- 4 croissants, split in half
- 6 slices of bacon, cooked and crumbled
- 1/2 cup of spinach, sautéed
- 1/2 cup of shredded cheese (cheddar, Swiss, or mozzarella)
- 2 eggs, scrambled
- Salt and pepper to taste

Instructions:

1. Preheat the oven to 375°F (190°C) and line a baking sheet with parchment paper.
2. Place the croissant halves on the baking sheet and toast in the oven for 5 minutes.
3. Scramble the eggs in a skillet over medium heat and season with salt and pepper.
4. Assemble the croissants by layering scrambled eggs, bacon, spinach, and cheese on each half.
5. Place them back in the oven for 5-7 minutes or until the cheese melts and everything is warmed through.
6. Serve immediately as a savory, satisfying breakfast.

Hot Spiced Apple Cider with Breakfast Biscuits

Ingredients:

- 4 cups of apple cider
- 2 cinnamon sticks
- 4 cloves
- 1 star anise
- 1 tablespoon of brown sugar
- 1 tablespoon of orange zest
- 1 batch of homemade or store-bought breakfast biscuits

Instructions:

1. In a large pot, heat apple cider with cinnamon sticks, cloves, star anise, and brown sugar over medium heat.
2. Bring to a simmer and cook for about 10 minutes, allowing the spices to infuse.
3. Add orange zest and stir well.
4. Remove from heat and strain out the spices before serving in mugs.
5. Serve hot with a side of warm breakfast biscuits.

Mushroom and Swiss Omelette

Ingredients:

- 2 large eggs
- 1/4 cup of milk
- 1/2 cup of sliced mushrooms
- 1/4 cup of shredded Swiss cheese
- 1 tablespoon of butter
- Salt and pepper to taste

Instructions:

1. Heat butter in a skillet over medium heat and sauté mushrooms until soft and browned.
2. Whisk together eggs, milk, salt, and pepper in a bowl.
3. Pour the egg mixture over the cooked mushrooms and cook until the edges begin to set.
4. Sprinkle the Swiss cheese over the omelette and fold it in half.
5. Cook for another 1-2 minutes until the cheese is melted and the eggs are fully set.
6. Serve immediately with toast or fresh herbs.

Oatmeal with Roasted Winter Squash

Ingredients:

- 1 cup of rolled oats
- 2 cups of milk (or dairy-free alternative)
- 1/2 cup of roasted winter squash (cubed)
- 1 tablespoon of maple syrup
- 1/2 teaspoon of cinnamon
- A pinch of nutmeg
- A handful of chopped nuts (optional)

Instructions:

1. In a medium saucepan, bring milk to a simmer and add oats.
2. Cook oats, stirring occasionally, until they reach a creamy consistency (about 5-7 minutes).
3. Stir in cinnamon, nutmeg, and maple syrup.
4. Top with roasted squash cubes and sprinkle with chopped nuts if desired.
5. Serve warm for a hearty, fall-inspired breakfast.

Hazelnut Coffee Cake

Ingredients:

- 2 cups of all-purpose flour
- 1/2 cup of sugar
- 1/2 cup of ground hazelnuts
- 1 teaspoon of baking powder
- 1/2 teaspoon of baking soda
- 1/2 cup of unsalted butter, softened
- 2 large eggs
- 1 cup of sour cream
- 1 teaspoon of vanilla extract
- A pinch of salt

Instructions:

1. Preheat the oven to 350°F (175°C) and grease a 9-inch round cake pan.
2. In a bowl, mix flour, sugar, ground hazelnuts, baking powder, baking soda, and salt.
3. In a separate bowl, cream together butter, eggs, sour cream, and vanilla extract.
4. Gradually add the dry ingredients to the wet ingredients and mix until smooth.
5. Pour the batter into the prepared pan and bake for 25-30 minutes, or until a toothpick comes out clean.
6. Cool slightly before serving with a dusting of powdered sugar or a glaze.

Warm Apple Cinnamon Polenta

Ingredients:

- 1 cup of cornmeal
- 4 cups of water or milk
- 1/4 cup of brown sugar
- 1 teaspoon of cinnamon
- 2 apples, peeled and diced
- 1 tablespoon of butter
- A pinch of salt

Instructions:

1. Bring water or milk to a boil in a medium saucepan, then add a pinch of salt.
2. Slowly whisk in cornmeal, stirring constantly to avoid lumps.
3. Reduce the heat to low and cook the polenta for about 15 minutes until thickened.
4. In a separate pan, sauté apples with butter and cinnamon until soft and caramelized.
5. Stir the brown sugar into the polenta and serve topped with the warm apples.
6. Enjoy this comforting breakfast with a drizzle of honey if desired.

Nutella-Stuffed Pancakes

Ingredients:

- 1 1/2 cups of all-purpose flour
- 1 tablespoon of sugar
- 1 teaspoon of baking powder
- 1/2 teaspoon of baking soda
- 1/2 teaspoon of salt
- 1 cup of buttermilk
- 1 large egg
- 2 tablespoons of melted butter
- Nutella for filling

Instructions:

1. In a large bowl, whisk together flour, sugar, baking powder, baking soda, and salt.
2. In a separate bowl, combine buttermilk, egg, and melted butter.
3. Pour the wet ingredients into the dry ingredients and stir until just combined.
4. Heat a griddle or skillet over medium heat and lightly grease with butter.
5. Pour 1/4 cup of batter onto the skillet and cook until bubbles form on the surface.
6. Add a spoonful of Nutella in the center and cover with more batter.
7. Flip the pancake and cook until golden brown. Serve with syrup and powdered sugar.

Cream Cheese-Stuffed Belgian Waffles

Ingredients:

- 2 cups of waffle mix (or homemade batter)
- 1/2 cup of cream cheese, softened
- 2 tablespoons of powdered sugar
- 1 teaspoon of vanilla extract
- Fresh berries for topping
- Maple syrup for serving

Instructions:

1. Preheat your waffle iron and grease with non-stick spray.
2. In a small bowl, mix cream cheese, powdered sugar, and vanilla extract until smooth.
3. Prepare the waffle batter according to the package instructions or your recipe.
4. Spoon a small amount of cream cheese mixture into the center of each waffle before closing the iron.
5. Cook the waffles until golden and crispy.
6. Serve topped with fresh berries and a drizzle of maple syrup.

Buttermilk Biscuits with Gravy

Ingredients:

- 1 batch of homemade or store-bought buttermilk biscuits
- 1/2 pound of sausage (bulk or links, crumbled)
- 2 tablespoons of flour
- 2 cups of milk
- Salt and pepper to taste

Instructions:

1. Bake the biscuits according to your recipe or package instructions.
2. In a skillet, cook the sausage over medium heat until browned.
3. Stir in flour and cook for another 1-2 minutes to form a roux.
4. Slowly add milk while stirring to avoid lumps, and cook until thickened.
5. Season with salt and pepper to taste.
6. Serve the gravy over the warm biscuits.

Warm Cinnamon Sugar Donuts

Ingredients:

- 1 cup of all-purpose flour
- 1/2 teaspoon of baking powder
- 1/2 teaspoon of cinnamon
- 1/4 teaspoon of salt
- 1/4 cup of sugar
- 1/4 cup of milk
- 1 large egg
- 2 tablespoons of melted butter
- 1/4 cup of cinnamon sugar (for coating)

Instructions:

1. Preheat your oven to 350°F (175°C) and grease a donut pan.
2. In a bowl, mix flour, baking powder, cinnamon, salt, and sugar.
3. In a separate bowl, whisk together milk, egg, and melted butter.
4. Stir the wet ingredients into the dry ingredients and mix until smooth.
5. Spoon the batter into the donut pan and bake for 12-15 minutes or until golden.
6. Let the donuts cool slightly before tossing them in cinnamon sugar. Serve warm.

Almond Joy Smoothie Bowl

Ingredients:

- 1 frozen banana
- 1/2 cup of almond milk (or milk of choice)
- 1/4 cup of Greek yogurt
- 2 tablespoons of cocoa powder
- 1 tablespoon of almond butter
- 1 tablespoon of shredded coconut
- 2 tablespoons of sliced almonds
- 1 teaspoon of honey or maple syrup

Instructions:

1. In a blender, combine frozen banana, almond milk, Greek yogurt, cocoa powder, and almond butter. Blend until smooth and creamy.
2. Pour the smoothie into a bowl and top with shredded coconut, sliced almonds, and a drizzle of honey or maple syrup.
3. Serve immediately for a fun and indulgent breakfast treat.

Roasted Pears with Greek Yogurt and Honey

Ingredients:

- 4 pears, halved and cored
- 1 tablespoon of olive oil
- 1 teaspoon of cinnamon
- 1 tablespoon of honey
- 1/2 cup of Greek yogurt
- Crushed walnuts for topping (optional)

Instructions:

1. Preheat your oven to 375°F (190°C). Place pear halves on a baking sheet.
2. Drizzle with olive oil and sprinkle with cinnamon.
3. Roast for 25-30 minutes until pears are soft and golden brown.
4. Serve each pear half with a spoonful of Greek yogurt, drizzle with honey, and top with crushed walnuts for added crunch.

Savory Avocado and Spinach Smoothie

Ingredients:

- 1/2 ripe avocado
- 1/2 cup of spinach
- 1/2 cup of unsweetened almond milk
- 1 tablespoon of chia seeds
- 1/2 teaspoon of lemon juice
- Salt and pepper to taste

Instructions:

1. In a blender, combine avocado, spinach, almond milk, chia seeds, and lemon juice.
2. Blend until smooth and creamy.
3. Season with salt and pepper to taste.
4. Serve in a glass and enjoy as a refreshing, savory smoothie.

Maple Bacon and Cheddar Breakfast Quiche

Ingredients:

- 1 pre-made pie crust
- 4 eggs
- 1/2 cup of heavy cream
- 1/2 cup of cheddar cheese, shredded
- 4 strips of bacon, cooked and crumbled
- 1 tablespoon of maple syrup
- Salt and pepper to taste

Instructions:

1. Preheat the oven to 375°F (190°C).
2. In a bowl, whisk together eggs, heavy cream, cheddar cheese, crumbled bacon, maple syrup, salt, and pepper.
3. Pour the mixture into the pie crust and bake for 30-35 minutes, or until the quiche is set and slightly golden.
4. Let cool for 10 minutes before slicing and serving.

Lemon and Blueberry Ricotta Pancakes

Ingredients:

- 1 cup of all-purpose flour
- 1/2 cup of ricotta cheese
- 1/2 cup of milk
- 2 large eggs
- 1 teaspoon of baking powder
- 1/2 teaspoon of lemon zest
- 1/2 cup of fresh blueberries
- 2 tablespoons of butter (for cooking)

Instructions:

1. In a bowl, whisk together flour, ricotta cheese, milk, eggs, baking powder, and lemon zest until smooth.
2. Gently fold in blueberries.
3. Heat a skillet over medium heat and add a little butter.
4. Pour batter onto the skillet, forming pancakes. Cook for 2-3 minutes on each side, until golden brown.
5. Serve with maple syrup and extra blueberries for a fresh breakfast treat.

Hot Buttered Rum Oatmeal

Ingredients:

- 1 cup of rolled oats
- 2 cups of water or milk
- 1 tablespoon of butter
- 1 tablespoon of brown sugar
- 1 teaspoon of cinnamon
- 1/4 teaspoon of nutmeg
- A splash of rum extract (or real rum for a fun twist)
- Chopped pecans or walnuts for topping (optional)

Instructions:

1. In a saucepan, bring water or milk to a boil and add oats.
2. Reduce the heat to low and simmer for 5-7 minutes, stirring occasionally.
3. Stir in butter, brown sugar, cinnamon, nutmeg, and rum extract.
4. Serve hot, topped with chopped nuts for an extra crunch.

Toasted Bagels with Smoked Salmon

Ingredients:

- 2 bagels, halved and toasted
- 4 ounces of smoked salmon
- 1/4 cup of cream cheese
- 1 tablespoon of capers
- 1/4 red onion, thinly sliced
- Fresh dill for garnish
- Lemon wedges for serving

Instructions:

1. Toast the bagel halves until golden brown.
2. Spread cream cheese on each bagel half.
3. Top with smoked salmon, capers, red onion, and a few sprigs of fresh dill.
4. Serve with a wedge of lemon on the side for extra brightness.

Cranberry Walnut Granola with Yogurt

Ingredients:

- 1 cup of rolled oats
- 1/2 cup of walnuts, chopped
- 1/4 cup of dried cranberries
- 2 tablespoons of honey
- 2 tablespoons of coconut oil
- 1 cup of plain Greek yogurt

Instructions:

1. Preheat the oven to 350°F (175°C). In a bowl, mix oats, chopped walnuts, and dried cranberries.
2. In a separate bowl, combine honey and coconut oil. Pour over the oat mixture and toss until evenly coated.
3. Spread the granola mixture on a baking sheet and bake for 15-20 minutes, stirring halfway through.
4. Once the granola is golden and crisp, remove from the oven and let it cool.
5. Serve the granola over a bowl of plain Greek yogurt for a nutritious and satisfying breakfast.

Chia Seed Pudding with Ginger Pear Compote

Ingredients:

- 3 tablespoons of chia seeds
- 1 cup of almond milk (or milk of choice)
- 1 tablespoon of maple syrup
- 2 pears, peeled and chopped
- 1 teaspoon of fresh ginger, grated
- 1 tablespoon of honey

Instructions:

1. In a bowl, combine chia seeds, almond milk, and maple syrup. Stir well and refrigerate for at least 4 hours or overnight.
2. In a saucepan, combine chopped pears, grated ginger, and honey. Cook over medium heat until the pears soften and release juice, about 10 minutes.
3. Serve the chia seed pudding topped with the ginger pear compote for a cozy, warming breakfast.

Breakfast Potatoes with Sweet Bell Peppers

Ingredients:

- 4 medium potatoes, diced
- 1 red bell pepper, diced
- 1 yellow bell pepper, diced
- 1 onion, diced
- 1 tablespoon of olive oil
- 1/2 teaspoon of paprika
- Salt and pepper to taste
- Fresh parsley for garnish

Instructions:

1. Heat olive oil in a large skillet over medium heat. Add diced potatoes and cook until golden and tender, about 10 minutes.
2. Add the diced bell peppers and onion, and cook for an additional 5-7 minutes until vegetables are softened.
3. Season with paprika, salt, and pepper. Stir to combine.
4. Garnish with fresh parsley and serve as a hearty breakfast side.

Hot Apple and Almond Butter Slices

Ingredients:

- 2 apples, cored and sliced
- 1/4 cup of almond butter
- 1 teaspoon of cinnamon
- 1 tablespoon of honey (optional)
- Chopped almonds for topping (optional)

Instructions:

1. In a skillet, heat the apple slices over medium heat until they soften and slightly caramelize, about 5 minutes.
2. Serve the warm apple slices with a dollop of almond butter on top.
3. Sprinkle with cinnamon, drizzle with honey (if desired), and top with chopped almonds for a delightful breakfast treat.

Cinnamon Spiced Dutch Baby Pancakes

Ingredients:

- 3 large eggs
- 1/2 cup of milk
- 1/2 cup of all-purpose flour
- 1/4 teaspoon of cinnamon
- 1/4 teaspoon of vanilla extract
- 2 tablespoons of butter
- Powdered sugar for serving
- Fresh berries for topping

Instructions:

1. Preheat the oven to 425°F (220°C). In a blender, combine eggs, milk, flour, cinnamon, and vanilla. Blend until smooth.
2. In a 10-inch cast-iron skillet, melt butter over medium heat. Once the butter is melted, pour the batter into the skillet.
3. Bake in the preheated oven for 20-25 minutes until the edges are golden and the center is puffed.
4. Dust with powdered sugar and top with fresh berries before serving.

www.ingramcontent.com/pod-product-compliance
Lightning Source LLC
LaVergne TN
LVHW081334060526
838201LV00055B/2639